Noah's Ark and the Lost World

Copyright © 1988, Institute for Creation Research

MASTER BOOKS

A Division of Creation Life Publishers

P.O. Box 1606

El Cajon, California 92022

Library of Congress Catalog Card Number 88 -

ISBN 0-89051-138-1

Cataloging in Publication Data

Morris, John D. , 1946 -
Noah's ark and the lost world.
1. History—Juvenile literature.
2. Noah's flood.

First Printing - October 1988
Second Printing - April 1989
Third Printing - March 1990
Fourth Printing - June 1991
Fifth Printing - September 1992

Printed in Hong Kong

FOREWORD

In recent years, mankind has begun to explore the moon, the solar system, and the universe around him. Many new discoveries are being made every day with the help of powerful telescopes that reach far into space, and plans are being made now to explore the stars even further.

But even though we are continually learning more about outer space and our own solar system, there is still much we don't know about the earth and its past. Was the earth once covered by water? Did Noah really build the Ark and take the animals on board to escape the Flood? And if so, what does it mean to us today?

To find answers to questions like these, I have become involved in one of the most exciting adventures possible: The search for Noah's Ark!

Walking on the moon made me more aware of the beauty of the earth and its God-given, created ability to support life—while walking on Mt. Ararat made me more aware of God's protection of His people in this world and His judgment of sin, not only for the people of Noah's day, but the people of our day as well.

I have been involved in the search for the Ark since 1982, while Dr. John Morris has been involved since 1971. John's background in geology allows him to understand the effects of the Flood on the earth and Mt. Ararat, and he knows nearly all there is to know about the search for Noah's Ark. His personal experiences on Mt. Ararat, including being struck by lightning, are truly thrilling.

In this book, John presents a Biblical view of the Flood and the earth's past, as well as its wonderful future, in addition to describing the search for the Ark. Most importantly, he has explained the message of Noah's Ark in a much-needed true story that will benefit everyone who reads it.

Noah's Ark and the Lost World is one of the most accurate, entertaining, and educational books available for would-be explorers of all ages....Readers will enjoy it again and again.

As part of the 1971 Apollo 15 Space Mission, Col. Irwin was the eighth man to walk on the moon

Col. Jim Irwin
Ararat Explorer and
NASA Astronaut

3

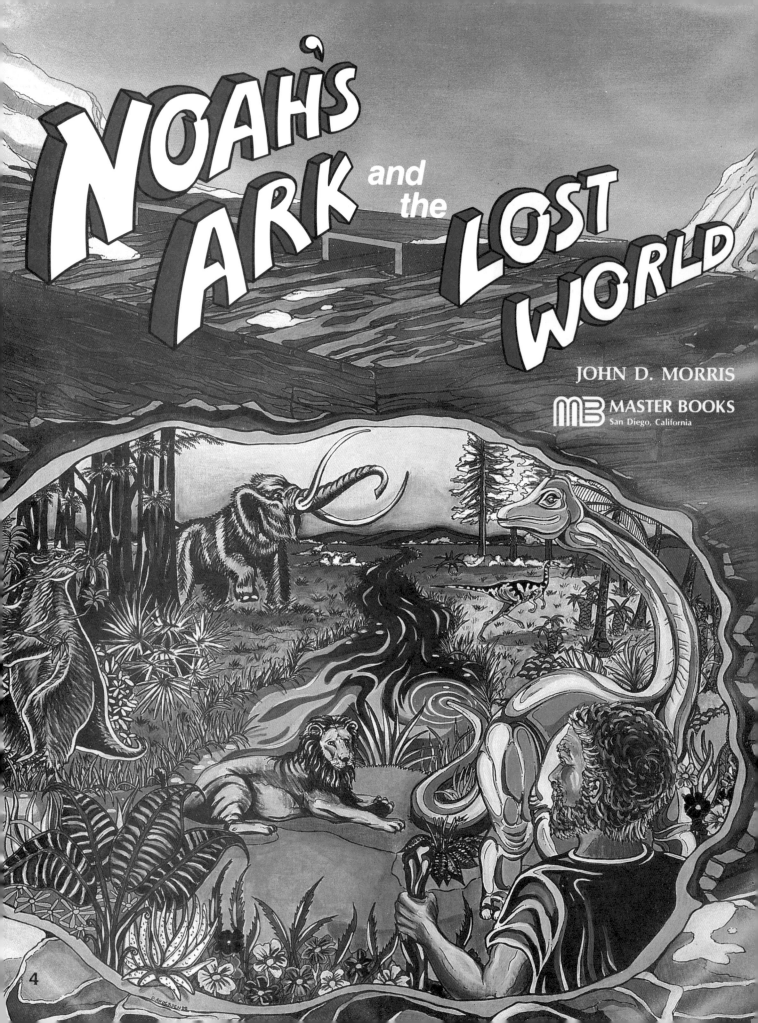

NOAH'S ARK and the LOST WORLD

JOHN D. MORRIS

MB MASTER BOOKS
San Diego, California

4

TABLE OF CONTENTS

CHAPTER 1

THE LOST WORLD

Imagine that you could visit the world as it was before the Great Flood of Noah's time. Imagine that the sun is just peeking over the horizon. It is morning in the forest. The animals are starting to move out of their dens, nests, and burrows where they have been sleeping. Their movements are joined by those of the night animals returning to their homes.

The search for food is not hard for these animals. The forest is rich with many kinds of plants that can be used for food, and there are plenty of smaller animals to be hunted. In the forest, trees, shrubs, and many colored flowers are abundant. Plants and animals in this forest are great in number and variety. This forest is very different from the forests that you can visit today.

As the morning mist rises from the ground, songs of birds join the other forest sounds. But if you listen closely, you will also hear strange sounds that you have never heard before. Over in a sandy clearing by a stream you can hear the peaceful clucking of a mother duck-billed dinosaur as she takes care of her newly hatched babies. Suddenly, you are startled by a deep roar from within a dense jungle of giant ferns and thick vines. It's the call of a sabre-toothed tiger, a giant cat with long curved teeth. The roar reminds you that this is also a world full of violence.

Leaving the forest, you move toward the grassy plains. There are tents in the distance. As you approach you can hear the sound of sheep and cattle. In the camp, men and women are beginning their morning work. Some of the older children are shouting while they chase away a family of small chicken-size dinosaurs from a garden near one of the tents. Nearby, a young man checks the thorn barrier protecting the newborn lambs and calves huddled close to their mothers. These people are related to a man named Jabal (Genesis 4:20). It is even possible that this is his camp.

Far off in the distance is a great city. Outside the city you see many small farms growing all kinds of plants that are good for food. Although people work in the fields, most of them want to spend the night within the safety of the city. Behind the city wall there are many houses—and each house looks like it is built to protect the family within from its neighbors. This city was built by a man named Cain and is named after his first son (Genesis 3:17).

From somewhere in the city comes music played on a flute and a harp. The

musicians were taught by Jubal, who is the inventor of these musical instruments (Genesis 4:21). It must be a party, but from the sound of the arguing it doesn't sound like much fun. From another part of the city comes a different sound, the clang of hammers beating hot iron and bronze into weapons and tools. This place belongs to Tubal-cain whose father brags, ''I have killed a man for wounding me and a young man for hurting me!'' (Genesis 4:22-23).

The violence and the wickedness of this world have not gone unnoticed by God. The Creator is sorry that He has made man on the earth, and His heart is broken by the evil that He sees. Soon God will destroy this world, and every person and every

The Bible tells us about the world in the beginning. God tells us the Bible is true (II Timothy 3:16,17). What if the Bible doesn't agree with what some people say about what happened long ago? We can choose to believe what was written by the One who was there, who is also the One who knows everything. Or we can believe people who were not there in the beginning and who do not know everything!

animal will be destroyed as well. But one man, Noah, along with his family, has obeyed God, and they will be saved (Genesis 6-8).

HOW CAN WE KNOW WHAT THE WORLD WAS LIKE BEFORE THE FLOOD?

How do we know anything about the past—the time before we were living? We can learn from people who recorded what the past was like. Sometimes they leave records that truthfully tell what the past was like, but sometimes they don't. The story of the Flood is like that. The Bible records the true account of what happened; but there are also many legends told by people who changed the real Flood story to fit their own purposes. Today many people don't know why the Flood happened and most are even told that it didn't happen at all.

There is other evidence of what happened in the past, although it is usually not as clear as the truthful records of people who were actually there. Fossils are one such kind of evidence. Have you ever seen layers of rocks with fossils of plants and animals inside? You probably have. Billions and billions of fossils have been found all over the world. There are billions and billions of fossils that have not yet been found, and there are billions and billions of fossils that will never be found! What caused all of these fossils?

In most cases fossils are the bodies of animals and plants that died when they were suddenly buried in mud. The mud later dried and became hard rock, keeping the shape—or even actual parts—of the plant or animal saved in stone. But what caused all the mud? The best answer is Noah's Flood, and when we see fossils, we should remember the Flood and why God sent it.

If we refuse to believe the details that God has provided in His Bible, then it becomes much harder to understand the past from the evidence that we see around us. It is like trying to know what a jigsaw puzzle looks like with only a small number of pieces. God has told us what the world was like before the Flood, and now the pieces of evidence that we find can begin to make sense.

Trying to understand the past from a few fossils that are dug up is like trying to put a puzzle together without knowing what picture is on the puzzle and without having all the pieces. You'll probably never get it right! But with the true history of the world given to us in the Bible, we CAN understand the fossils and the past. Most fossils were laid down by the horrible Flood recorded in Genesis.

THE WORLD IN THE BEGINNING

In the beginning the world was different from the world that was destroyed by the Flood. The Bible says that Adam and Eve, the first two people God made, walked with God in the Garden of Eden. From the description of this perfect world in the book of Genesis, we know that no place as beautiful as this exists on earth today (Genesis 2).

The animals lived in peace with man and with one another. Adam and Eve did not kill animals for meat. They ate from the plants and fruits of the Garden, as did all of the animals that were created then. Adam and Eve were made so that they would never get sick, and certainly never die. Every day was sunshine and cloudless skies because there was no rain. A mist would come up from the ground and water the many plants in the Garden. It was a time of health and happiness (Genesis 2:5-6).

Adam and Eve also had plenty of work to do. They were responsible for caring for the Garden and the animals that shared Eden with them. But God also gave Adam and Eve a warning, which gave them an opportunity to obey Him. He told them not to eat the fruit from a certain tree—the one that He called the "Tree of Knowledge of Good and Evil." God told them that if they ate fruit from this tree, then they would begin to die! (Genesis 2:15-17).

There were many other delicious fruits, nuts, and vegetables in the Garden of which they could eat. But God wanted to see if they would be obedient. You see, God had given Adam and Eve everything that they needed to have a perfect life so they would never die. Now it was up to our first parents, Adam and Eve, to obey their Creator or to rebel against Him. It would be their choice.

ADAM AND EVE CHOOSE

Genesis tells us that there was another creature in the Garden. This creature, named Satan, hated God, not because of anything that his Creator had done to him, but because he wanted to be like God and rule in God's place (Isaiah 14:13-14).

One day Satan, secretly using the body of a snake, found Eve near the forbidden tree. He told her lies and changed the meaning of what God had told her. Satan said that the tree would make her just as wise as God. He told her that she would not die, and that God didn't want her to eat the fruit of the tree because He did not want her to be equal to Him (Genesis 3:1-5).

Eve saw that the tree's fruit looked good and thought that it would be good to eat. And she wanted to be just as wise as God. Eve decided to disobey God and ate the fruit. Once she had eaten the fruit, she took some to Adam. Satan did not need to deceive Adam into disobeying. Even though God had been so good to them, Adam chose to rebel against the one rule that God had given him.

Of course, the fruit did not make them wise like God. In fact, it made them realize how foolish and small they really were. They knew that they had disobeyed and, to make things worse, they tried to hide their disobedience from God. They knew that God hates sin and would have to judge and punish their sin of disobedience. And He had promised that the punishment would be death! (Genesis 3:6-13).

THE PROMISE

But even though God had to punish their sin, He loved Adam and Eve. He wanted them to ask for forgiveness and to be friends with Him again. So he told them of a marvelous plan. He promised that one day a woman would have a Son who would take their punishment for them. When that Son grew to be a man, even though He would be wounded by Satan, still He would conquer Satan, ending the

evil and death caused by sin. This Savior, promised by God to Eve and Adam so long ago, is Jesus Christ, God's Son, who died on the cross as a punishment for their sin (and our sin also) (Genesis 3:15) and rose from the dead in victory over Satan.

Because Adam and Eve were responsible for caring for the creation, their sin also brought death into the world (Romans 5:12; I Cor. 15:21). They were driven out of the beautiful Garden. Until Eden was later destroyed by the Flood, an angel was sent to guard the Garden and keep anyone from returning to it.

THE EFFECTS OF SIN

Outside of the Garden, Adam and Eve found that the world had changed. They had to work very hard to grow and gather their food. Some plants grew thorns and others could not be eaten. No longer were Adam and Eve able to live peacefully with all of the animals. Worst of all, every living thing began to die. Through violence, sickness, or old age, each person and each animal would die (Genesis 3:14-24).

All of these things reminded Adam and Eve how horrible sin really is. And each time they would see a meat-eating animal make its kill, or touch a plant with thorns, or have to work hard, or see someone die, they would remember that the God who loved them and who had given them only good things, also had to punish them for their disobedience.

As time went on, Adam and Eve had sons and daughters and their children had more sons and daughters. At the first, of course, brothers and sisters had to marry each other, but this was not a problem until much later, when the effects of sin on our bodies were much greater (Genesis 5:4).

11

Sooner or later everything died, but most things lived a long time and many things grew to large sizes. Adam lived for almost a thousand years after his creation (Genesis 5:5). In fact, it was not until after the Flood that God allowed the life of humans to last only about 70 years or so (Psalms 90:10). Likewise, all of Adam and Eve's children, grandchildren, great-grand-children, great-great-grandchildren, and so on, also lived long lives. Even though sin had changed the world, it was still a more pleasant place to live when compared with the world today. There were still no storms and many animals were peaceful.

But each day people became more disobedient. Before long, people everywhere laughed at the idea of obeying God. By their violent and wicked lives, they showed that they hated God. There were still some people who loved God, but they were few. The people who still loved God tried to get the others to come back to God, but the people would not listen (Genesis 4:26; 5:22 and Jude 14-15).

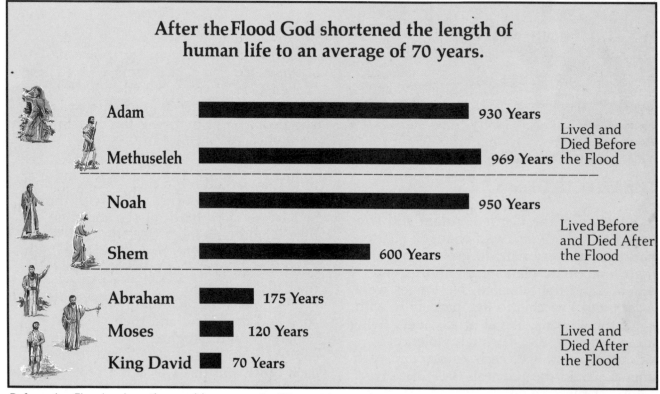

After the Flood God shortened the length of human life to an average of 70 years.

Adam		930 Years	Lived and Died Before the Flood
Methuseleh		969 Years	
Noah		950 Years	Lived Before and Died After the Flood
Shem		600 Years	
Abraham		175 Years	
Moses		120 Years	Lived and Died After the Flood
King David		70 Years	

Before the Flood, when the world was much different than today, people sometimes lived almost one thousand years! But after the Flood, people's lives were much shorter. Today, few people even live to 100 years old.

THE LOST WORLD PUNISHED

The Bible says that "the earth was filled with violence" (Genesis 6:13). Even the animals were living in a way that did not please their Creator. Everything that breathed had been changed by sin. If God had not acted to destroy the earth, then even the few men and women who still obeyed Him would have been lost, and the Savior, who had been promised, could not have been born.

But God does not punish those who trust in Him. Noah and his family loved and trusted God, and God warned them of His plan to destroy the world. He told Noah to build an Ark, a huge boat, big enough to provide safety for his family and every kind of animal that lived on the land. It probably took Noah nearly 120 years to build the Ark (Genesis 6:3). During that time no one else began to love the Lord (Hebrews 11:7). Noah told the people that

God was going to send a Flood to destroy the world and everything in it, but no one listened. He said that if they believed and obeyed God, then they could find safety on the Ark, but they only made fun of him. The people kept on living the way that they wanted (II Peter 2:5).

The end of this Lost World came suddenly. Seven days after Noah and his family were safely inside the Ark with the animals, rain began to fall (Genesis 7:10). It was not a gentle rain, but rain and hail so powerful that it destroyed life. The people had never seen rain. Perhaps they quickly realized that the destruction about which Noah had warned them was beginning. But even if they did, it was too late. God had already closed the Ark to protect the people and animals inside (Genesis 7:16). Outside of the Ark terrified people and animals would try to seek safety, but their opportunity to be saved was lost.

13

CHAPTER 2

THE ARK AND THE FLOOD

Noah's Ark was not a small boat. In fact, it was longer than a football field and taller than a four-story building. The measurements that God gave to Noah were in "cubits," a Hebrew measurement used at that time which was the distance from a man's elbow to the tip of his fingers, or about 18 inches (about 0.45 meters).

When the measurements of the Ark in Genesis 6:15 are changed to feet, we discover the Ark was about 450 feet long (135 meters), 75 feet wide (23 meters), and 45 feet tall (13 meters). Compare this with the big truck in the picture and imagine how many truckloads of animals and other supplies could be loaded into the Ark!

Some people think that the Ark was too small to carry all of the pairs of animals on board, but most of these people have not taken the time to look at just how big the Ark really was. It is easy to see that there was room for everything, and simple math shows us there was even extra space left over.

Many story books show pictures of the Ark as some kind of houseboat with a few animals on board sticking their heads out the top, but this is certainly not right. The Bible describes Noah's Ark as HUGE! The Ark's "tonnage," or the amount of weight it could carry, was nearly *forty million pounds (fifteen million kilograms)!* It probably looked much more like a giant cargo ship or enclosed barge, all sealed up tight for protection against the terrible storm to come.

Was Noah's Ark a small boat full of happy animals, or was it more like a huge floating warehouse? The Ark on the left is like the kind you see in most stories. The modern truck in the picture above (just for comparison) shows the great size of the real Ark, as described in the Bible.

HOW COULD NOAH BUILD SUCH A BOAT?

Noah and his three sons probably had close to 120 years to build the Ark (Genesis 6:3). The people who lived then were very skilled workers who were able to make almost anything they could imagine, but of course for this project, Noah and his sons followed directions from God. Even if they had never built a ship before, they were probably pretty good carpenters after a year or two. There was plenty of time for them to cut down trees, make lumber, and finish construction on the Ark.

God told Noah to make three decks in the Ark with rooms that could be used for animal stalls and storage (Genesis 6:14, 16). God also told Noah to cover the Ark inside and out with some kind of ''pitch'' to keep water from leaking into the rooms.

Noah and his sons may have had a special recipe to cook the pitch, much like the tar we use today for roof repair. This same pitch might also have helped keep the Ark from rotting and being destroyed by the weather after it landed on Mt. Ararat.

HOW DID NOAH GET ALL THE ANIMALS?

Noah and his family did not have to gather the animals themselves. The Bible says that God brought all the animals to Noah in time to get on board (Genesis 6:19-20).

Because all kinds of animals lived much closer together before the Flood, they probably did not have to travel far to get to the Ark. (The world looked much different then, with no high mountains to divide the land and no great oceans to divide the continents). It was much easier for people and animals to get from place to place than it is today.

HOW COULD ALL THE ANIMALS FIT INSIDE THE ARK?

Pairs of each "kind," or basic type of land-dwelling, air-breathing animal, had to be on board the Ark (Genesis 7:22). We don't know how many such kinds were alive in Noah's day, but today there are less than 20,000 different types of animals, not counting those animals who live in the sea, or those who don't breath air. Even most insects were probably not on the Ark. They don't "breathe" air and their eggs and larvae would survive on floating logs outside the Ark.

All modern types could have come from about 5,000 kinds or less that God originally created. But no matter how many kinds there were, we know that the Ark was big enough to haul more than 50,000 animals, with room to spare!

Although there were no doubt many daily chores to do during the months of the Flood, most of the animals would have required very little care. Many animals (like bears) hibernate when the weather is bad, and almost every creature will lie very quiet and still when trapped during times of great danger.

The great storm would have been very frightening, with great winds howling, thunder and lightning crashing, and waves pounding all day and all night; but the "survival instincts" that God created within the animals would have kept them rather peaceful through the tossing and rolling of the Ark during the horrible storm.

WHAT DID THE ANIMALS EAT ON THE ARK?

God told Noah to take food on the Ark for the animals and his family (Genesis 6:21). Certainly the animals would not be allowed to eat each other, and they would not be fighting during this time of danger anyway. There was probably food like hay and corn on board, but because many animals were in a hibernation-like state, Noah and his family did not have to feed them very much at all.

WHAT ABOUT THE DINOSAURS?

All of the various kinds of land dinosaurs were on the Ark with the rest of the animals. After all, God created them on Day Six along with Adam and Eve. And when God brought two animals of *every* kind to board the Ark, the dinosaurs must have been included too! We know that dinosaurs not only lived along with man before the Flood, but also survived the Flood to live afterward with man.

Sometime we think about dinosaurs as being vicious, mean beasts, but when God created the world, all animals were to live in peace with each other and with man. Originally, dinosaurs and other creatures ate only plants (Genesis 1:29-30). Today, animals that eat only plants are called ''herbivores.''

It may be that after Adam and Eve sinned, some of the dinosaurs and other animals became meat-eaters (or ''carnivores''), but we do not know exactly when or if this actually happened. Some fossil bones of dinosaurs do look like they belong to ''terrible lizards,'' but there is no way to know for sure how the great creatures behaved toward each other. All we find are bones of dead ones!

17

God felt that these powerful creatures were quite special. In the book of Job, the Bible describes two great beasts that we would call "dinosaurs" today. The people of Job's day (who lived soon after the Flood) called one of these animals "Behemoth." We can read about God's description of the power and majesty of this awesome creature in Job 40:15-24. The other dinosaur is called "Leviathan" and breathes out smoke and fire like a dragon. You can read about this fearsome marine-dwelling creature in Job Chapter 41.

After reading these verses, what kind of dinosaurs do you think Behemoth and Leviathan were? God calls Behemoth "chief among His works," or in other words, "king of the land animals."

The description God gave to Job sounds like a very large and powerful dinosaur, with legs like iron and a tail as large and long as a tall cedar tree. This creature might be an *Apatosaurus* or *Brachiosaurus*, an animal that could weigh up to 33 tons and eat 2,000 pounds of green plants every day!

Most dinosaurs were not as big as this giant, however, and God did not need to bring full-grown animals into the Ark. Usually reptiles (including dinosaurs) grow bigger and bigger as long as they live, but Noah probably took young, strong dinosaurs on the Ark—ones much smaller than fully grown dinosaurs. (Modern reptiles, even if they grew to be very old, would not be dinosaurs. Dinosaurs had different hip joints and skull types than any modern reptile.)

OUTSIDE THE ARK

God sent the Flood as a judgment against the evil, wicked, and violent people of the earth. All the people died. All the land animals died. Many, but not all fish and other ocean creatures died also. All land creatures that had the breath of life in them were wiped from the face of the earth...all except those on the Ark with Noah and his family (Genesis 7:22-23).

Outside the Ark, after Noah and his family got on board and God closed the door, the wicked people probably continued to make fun of Noah and shout insults at him...until it began to rain. They had never seen it rain before—and no one today has seen it rain as hard as it rained during the first 40 days and 40 nights of Noah's Flood.

The Bible says on "on that day all the fountains of the great deep were broken up, and the windows of heaven were opened" (Genesis 7:11), meaning that all of the water below the earth and all of the water above the earth rushed to cover the earth.

20

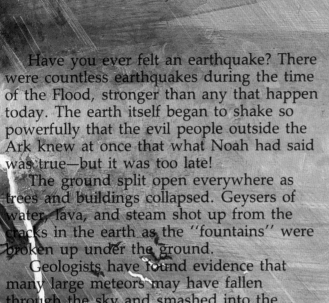

Have you ever felt an earthquake? There were countless earthquakes during the time of the Flood, stronger than any that happen today. The earth itself began to shake so powerfully that the evil people outside the Ark knew at once that what Noah had said was true—but it was too late!

The ground split open everywhere as trees and buildings collapsed. Geysers of water, lava, and steam shot up from the cracks in the earth as the "fountains" were broken up under the ground.

Geologists have found evidence that many large meteors may have fallen through the sky and smashed into the ground during this time as well. These huge rocks from space broke up the ground, causing earthquakes and destroying everything for miles around.

Huge walls of rushing water pounded the earth and swept away all that was left of great cities. The Ark did not seem to move at first, but as wave after wave rushed over the ground and crashed into its sides, the great Ark rose above the earth. You probably have been in a terrible rain storm before, but have you ever seen a tornado or huricane? This storm was the greatest hurricane in history!

Can you imagine being in the Ark, tossed back and forth and up and down as huge waves crashed about you? Although they were safe inside, Noah and his family probably held on to each other in fear, as if they were on a non-stop roller coaster ride!

We can be thankful that we have not seen or been in such a terrible storm.

Even after the Flood covered the earth, and the world became one great ocean, the volcanic eruptions continued beneath the water. The earth was being destroyed (II Peter 3:6). It would never again look the same as it did before the Flood.

Ronald Hight

HOW COULD THE FLOOD COVER TALL MOUNTAINS?

The water covered even the highest mountain, high enough for the Ark to float right over the top of it. The mountains we see today are higher than those that God made when He created the earth. We know this because most of today's mountains are made of many, many layers of mud, now turned to rock, stacked on top of each other by the waters of the Flood.

These layers were originally formed under water, as all of the dirt and rocks got sorted and sifted during the Flood and settled out flat on the bottom of the Flood ocean. Today we can see the layers packed together with billions and billions of fossils of creatures which died during the Flood. Bodies of dead plants and animals that were sloshed around and sorted by the waves were buried in these layers, which later dried out and became hard rock.

When these layers (also called "strata") were still soft mud, they could be bent like clay and pushed upward into huge mountains by earth movements during Noah's Flood. Many of the other tall mountains we see now are volcanoes which erupted and grew taller after the Flood was over, so we can see that even though today's mountains were made by the Flood, they were not as high during the Flood as they are now.

The Grand Canyon was not eroded by the Colorado River, which would not be able to carve hard rock into the shape we see it. Only a vast amount of water rushing over soft muddy deposits could carve out a canyon that looks like this. It probably happened near the end of Noah's Flood.

WHERE DID ALL THE WATER GO?

When God decided to end the Flood, He caused the deep ocean floors to form, perhaps by separating the continents. As the waters rushed off, the earth's new surface took shape. Huge canyons, like the Grand Canyon, were carved out of the soft earth by the water as it flowed off the land into the new ocean basins.

If the earth were still round and smooth, with no high mountains and no deep oceans, it would be covered nearly two miles deep with water, even today! Aren't you glad that the mountains are higher now than they were during the Flood?

23

THE WORLD AFTER THE FLOOD

Toward the end of the Flood, God caused the land to appear. Mountains were suddenly raised up out of the water, as large basins—which are now today's oceans—were made to hold the flood waters.

When you visit or look at pictures of the Grand Canyon, you can see layers upon layers of rocks that were once mud. These rock layers were laid down during Noah's Flood. The deep canyon was cut as the Flood waters raced off the land while the layers were still relatively soft, just like mud or sand can be easily eroded.

In parts of the world whole forests had been ripped out of the ground by the Flood waters. Parts of them were later buried to form large beds of coal, while other organisms were buried in such a way that they turned into oil and gas. These "fossil fuels" are the energy that we use today. The floating logs and plants which didn't get buried under the ground, landed on top of the ground as the waters drained away. Insect eggs on the logs hatched and seeds and sprigs began to sprout.

When the Ark settled on the mountain, Noah first sent out a raven to see if life outside the Ark was possible. It probably found floating bodies of animals to eat and didn't come back. Noah later sent out a dove, and still later another dove. When it returned, it had a small olive twig in its beak. Later, the dove was able to find a home outside the Ark, and Noah knew that it was safe to leave (Genesis 8:6-13).

We can only imagine what it was like in those days. At first, few things were growing and life was hard for Noah's family and the animals. But it was not long before fast-growing grasses and even flowers sprouted from the moist soil. Shrubs and trees scattered over the earth. Eventually, these plants provided food and homes for the different kinds of animals leaving the Ark.

BABYLON   GREECE   INDIA

Babylonian "gods" (idols) told a man to build a boat with nine decks and fill it with his family, property, cattle, wild beasts, and food. Life on earth was to be destroyed by a great flood. After rain lasting only six days, this Babylonian "Noah" sent out a dove, a swallow, and a raven. When he left the boat, he sacrificed an animal, and the gods were so pleased that they made the man and his wife gods also.

In an ancient Greek story a man made a box into which he put all the things necessary for life. When he and his wife shut themselves in the box, the Greek god Zeus caused a great rain to fall. Everyone died except those who climbed to the tops of very high mountains. For nine days and nights the man was tossed on the sea. Finally the box landed and he and his wife left the box.

An early story from India tells of a fish that warned a man called Manu about a flood that would kill everything. Like the true story, Manu was told to build a boat, but Manu alone survived the flood.

WHAT ABOUT THE PEOPLE?

When Noah, his family, and the animals left the Ark and offered a sacrifice to God, God spoke to Noah again. God told him that his sons, their children, and their children's children were to fill the whole earth. But after some time, the descendants of Noah's sons had only traveled a few hundred miles from where the Ark had landed. At this time all people had the same language. It was easy for them to work together and share the same ideas, and they decided to disobey God by not spreading across the earth as He had told them to do.

But this disobedience was not the only thing. Ruled by a strong leader named Nimrod, these people built many great cities and decided to build a great tower that would reach high into the heavens (Genesis 11:4). Nimrod led the people to worship the stars, in direct disobedience to God's command to worship Him. Today many people still worship the stars, even though God says it is sin.

God could see that these people were following the same path of disobedience as the people before the Flood, and that nothing they could imagine would be impossible for them to do (Genesis 11:6). But there was a way to stop them from finishing the tower. God gave each family a new language, different from what they had known before. When this happened, the people could not understand each other or work together and quit building the high tower. This unfinished structure was named the "Tower of Babel," meaning "Tower of Confusion." The families and groups that spoke each language left and began journeys to far parts of the earth (Genesis 11:7-9). Some groups soon started mighty nations in Egypt, China, near Israel, and elsewhere. Others lived in caves and jungles with very primitive cultures. God had forced them to fill the new earth, even though they had tried to disobey.

Wherever people went, they would tell their children the story of Noah and the Great Flood. As time went on, some story-tellers would add to or change the true story. Only God's Word, the Bible, still has the true story. Hundreds of such Flood stories told by people at different times, and in different parts of the world, have been collected. Here are a few that show how the true Biblical story has been changed.

NORTH AMERICA   SOUTH AMERICA   THE PACIFIC

In North America, the Lenni Lenape Indians told of a time when a powerful snake made all people wicked. The snake caused water to destroy everything. But on an island was a man named Manabozho, the grandfather of all men. He was saved by riding on the back of a great turtle, not in the Ark like in the true story.

From Peru a story comes about a shepherd and his family. They noticed one day that their llamas were sad, so they studied to find out why. The stars told about a great flood which was coming. The shepherd and his family climbed a high mountain, and as the water rose higher and higher, the top of the mountain began to float so that they were saved.

Even the islands of the Pacific have flood stories. One of these explains how a fisherman got his fishing hook caught in the hair of the ocean god. The god awoke and decided that people were evil and should be destroyed. The fisherman begged for forgiveness, so the god told him to go to an island where he would be safe from the flood he would send.

CHAPTER 3

THE ARK AND THE MOUNTAIN

The Bible doesn't say what happened to the Ark after its landing on Mt. Ararat. Noah and his sons could have taken the Ark apart to build houses and shelters. Or, the Ark could have just turned into dust after many years.

But probably not. Since the time of the Flood, people all over the world have written or told stories about the Ark. There are many eyewitnesses who say they have seen the Ark while climbing on Mt. Ararat. Others say that they knew people who had seen the Ark. And in recent years many people claim to have seen the Ark from airplanes.

HOW COULD THE ARK BE PRESERVED?

Today the top of Mt. Ararat is covered with a glacier, a large area of snow and ice that never completely melts. It is possible that the Ark is in the glacier and can only be seen during the hottest summers, when much of the ice and snow melt away for a few weeks. Naturally, if the Ark is in a glacier, it would be frozen and could not rot. The Bible tells us that Noah put "pitch" all over the Ark, both inside and out. This covering of pitch would also help keep the Ark from rotting.

The Bible says "the Ark rested on the mountains of Ararat" (Genesis 8:4), or the region around the ancient country of "Urartu." Over the years hundreds of people claim to have seen Noah's Ark high on this mountain, which is called Mt. Ararat today. Most of them say that it is in or near the rocky canyon in this picture called the Ahora Gorge, up near the snow line.

Here is another idea to think about. Mt. Ararat is a volcano. It has erupted many times since the Flood. Sometimes red-hot rock, called lava, flowed out of the volcano. As the lava slowly moved along, it would have burned everything that it touched, including the Ark! However, when a volcano erupts, it does not always throw out lava. Many times, the volcano blows out great amounts of tiny pieces of dust, which would cover everything in sight. This dust is called volcanic ash. The dust is hot, but not hot enough to burn everything.

If the Ark were covered by a layer of volcanic ash, it would even have been protected from any burning lava which came later. After a long time the wood could even have turned into stone, or become petrified. Have you ever seen petrified wood? The best way for wood to turn to stone is for it to be covered by volcanic ash. Many of the people who say they have seen the Ark say it is as hard as stone.

These are two possible ways that the Ark might have been preserved all of these years. The Bible does not teach that the Ark would last, but many people have said that they have seen it. Perhaps some day soon someone will discover the Ark and solve the mystery!

HAVE PEOPLE REALLY SEEN NOAH'S ARK?

What an adventure it would be to explore the Ark! Think about climbing over the roof deck and looking into the windows along the top. Maybe you could get inside the Ark through one of these. Inside you might be able to explore the stalls where the animals were kept and wonder what kind of animals each had held. As you explore you might even find the rooms where Noah and his family stayed while the Flood waters raged against the Ark. Without doubt, finding Noah's Ark would be one of the major discoveries of our lifetime.

According to the people who live around Mt. Ararat today, 100 years ago people visited the Ark many times. Parents often took their children up to see the Ark and

explained the story of Noah and the Flood. Many other explorers, airplane pilots, travelers, and shepherds also claim to have seen the Ark. I have heard of and read many such stories and have talked to some of the people. Almost always their stories are very similar. Here are a few stories that are some of the most important.

EYEWITNESS STORIES

Around 1905 a shepherd boy named Jacob saw the Ark while trying to find his lost goats. Pictures that he drew show a box-like Ark sticking out of the ice. His drawings show the Ark resting on the edge of a steep drop-off. (Sketch A)

In 1908, and again in 1910, another shepherd boy whose name was Georgie climbed the mountain with his uncle to see

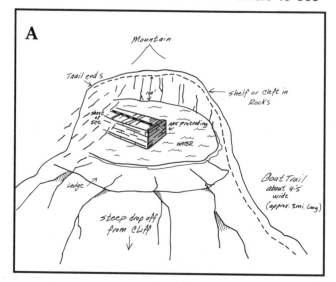

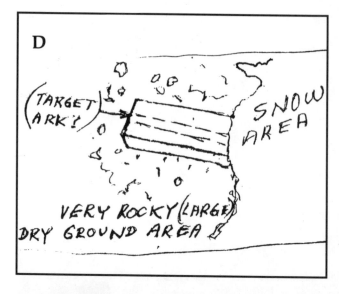

the Ark. He even walked on top of the Ark and looked inside the windows. They had to pile up rocks next to the Ark to get on top. Georgie said the Ark was as hard as rock and was covered with boulders and snow in some places. (Sketch B)

Often, great mystery surrounds stories about the Ark and the people who have seen it. In 1916 and 1917 soldiers and scientists from Russia climbed the mountain to see the Ark. They took photographs and drew maps of the Ark. They even went inside and saw stalls where the animals had been. While they were on the mountain, war started in their country, and when they returned home, the pictures were lost. Several of the scientists and soldiers traveled to other countries and were able to tell their stories, but they didn't have the photographs or maps as proof. Then, just a few years ago, an old Russian man suddenly appeared. He had photographs of the Ark, which he said were taken by the earlier explorers. He showed them to a man who sketched what was in the photographs, But now the mysterious Russian has died and the photographs have disappeared. Nobody knows where these pictures are, but they showed something like Sketch C.

Notice how similar all of these drawings are. They show a long, box-like boat with a long window along the top. In all of the drawings, the Ark looks different from any boats that the eyewitnesses would have seen or that we could see today. All of the witnesses say that only part of the Ark can be seen, with the rest of it still covered by rock, ice, and snow. They say it sits on a ledge, with a cliff rising on one side and a steep dropoff on the other.

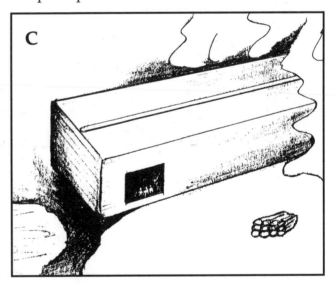

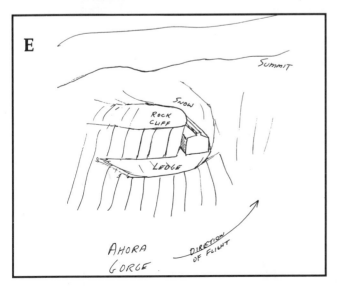

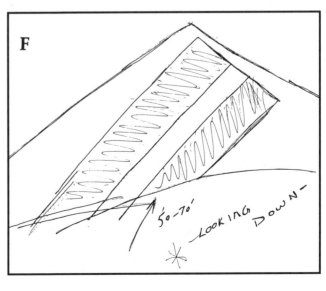

RECENT SIGHTINGS

Many people who are still living say that they have seen Noah's Ark from airplanes (Sketch D). Others have climbed to it. Many of them have drawn what they remembered and all of the drawings look very much the same. I have talked to several of these people and I believe that they are telling the truth.

Mr. Albert Shappell saw the Ark from a Navy airplane in 1974. He took pictures of the Ark, but was not allowed to keep them. He drew what he remembered (Sketch E). Also in 1974, Mr. Ed Behling saw the Ark. He was taken up to it by an old shepherd who lived on the mountain. He didn't take any pictures, but he recalls that the Ark was sticking out of the mountain, not out of the ice. He was not able to get all of the way down to it without ropes to help him, so he wasn't able to explore the Ark up close (Sketch F).

Usually, people remember details a little differently. As you can see, these drawings are all slightly different. Still, all of them are obviously describing the same thing, and all of the drawings agree with how the Bible describes the Ark (see Chapter 2).

The trouble with these stories is that none of the people have been able to tell exactly where they saw the Ark. Mt. Ararat is a huge and dangerous mountain. Even from the eyewitness accounts, we cannot be sure where to look.

The American spy-plane, the U-2, has taken pictures from the air which show the Ark, some people say. We can't get these secret photos from the government, but it has been drawn like this.

THE MYSTERY PHOTO

What do you see in this picture? A friend of mine took this photo by holding his camera out over the edge of a cliff. It was too dangerous for him to reach the edge and look over, but he was able to take several pictures of the hidden canyon below. When the film was developed and the pictures examined, a strange object that looks like Noah's Ark could be seen, just as these enlargements show. But because he didn't actually see the object himself, we don't know for certain what it really is. In fact, the more we study the picture, the less we believe it to be the Ark—but we certainly plan to go back and take a closer look! We call this picture the "Mystery Photo."

THE UNIDENTIFIED OBJECT

Look at the picture on the next page. The object that looks like Noah's Ark was not seen when the picture was taken. We have not been able to find the object again. We don't know for sure, but the object certainly looks like Noah's Ark! Several explorers think that this is a photograph of the Ark, but first we must find it again. We call it the "unidentified object."

Recently, I met a man named Mr. Ed Davis. Years ago, when he was a soldier in the U.S. Army, some of the local people near Mt. Ararat became his friends. Because of this friendship, they took him up on the mountain and showed him the Ark. Much later an artist named Elfred Lee listened to his story and carefully drew the picture on this page. Mr. Davis explained each detail as he remembers it. What is even more exciting is that he has also told us exactly how to get to the place where he says he saw the Ark. Next time we go to Mt.

Ararat, we have a good idea where to look.

Of course, we must be careful before we make too many conclusions about where the Ark will be found. It is possible for a rock or piece of ice to be in a box-like shape. We could make a mistake and think that we are seeing the Ark when we are not, if we are not careful. Again, it is important that those of us who are searching for Noah's Ark bring back certain proof of its discovery. But this is not easy. Many people who live near the mountain don't want us climbing "their mountain." Many times the local police or the Turkish Army do not want us to climb. And just climbing the mountain is very dangerous and difficult, so it is a big help to know where to look.

In recent years we have been able to use pictures taken by satellites in outer space to help us search for Noah's Ark. So far we haven't seen anything that we know is the Ark, but several interesting shapes can be seen that we want to climb to and study.

APPROVED
EYE WITNESS ACCOUNT – SEEN IN 1943
BY ED DAVIS – PERSONALLY TOLD TO, AND
DRAWN BY ELFRED LEE
6/15/86 ©

Mr. Ed Davis' description of the Ark, drawn by Elfred Lee. We have not yet been allowed to search in this area.

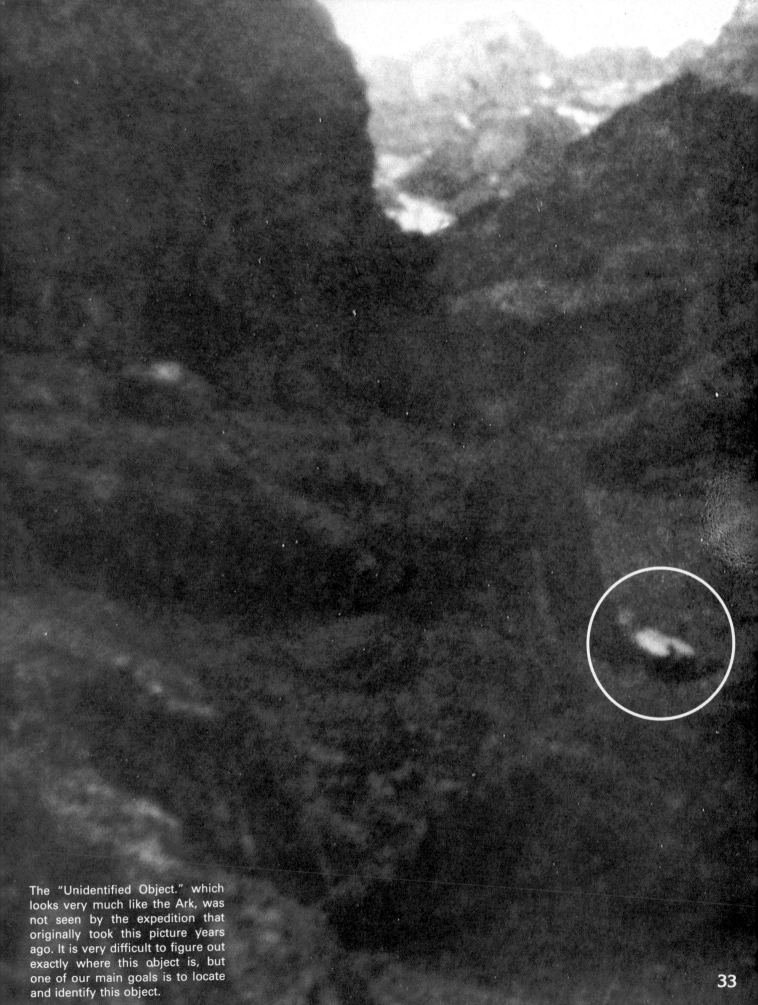

The "Unidentified Object." which looks very much like the Ark, was not seen by the expedition that originally took this picture years ago. It is very difficult to figure out exactly where this object is, but one of our main goals is to locate and identify this object.

CHAPTER 4

ADVENTURE ON ARARAT

Many people have gone to Mt. Ararat to try to find Noah's Ark. I have been there more than ten times.

The first time that I climbed Mt. Ararat, I was looking for the strange "unidentified object" in the picture on page 33. Because the glacier moves down the mountain and rocks of all sizes continually shift and move downhill, I did not know exactly where to look. The mountain changes a little each day of the year.

There are few mountains as dangerous to climb as Mt. Ararat. Things happened during each of my climbs to make me believe that Satan was trying to keep us from finding the Ark. Satan knows that if Noah's Ark is found, many people's eyes will be opened and they will believe the Bible.

DANGER!

Many times while climbing we were nearly hit by falling rocks. Some of these rocks were boulders bigger than a car. At times, hundreds of rocks would start rolling down the mountain as fast as a runaway truck. They would easily crush anyone they hit. Even the smaller rocks could kill. Some climbers have been seriously injured, and others even killed, on Mt. Ararat, but we are thankful that God has protected us and that none of the people climbing with me have ever been hit by these rockslides.

The ice and snow are also very dangerous. Sometimes deep caves are just beneath a thin snow cover, and if a climber fell into one, he might never get out. The ice also has cracks in it which are big enough for a man to fall into. Many climbers have fallen into these cracks; some have suffered broken bones, and others have died. Often snow and ice break loose from the top of the mountain and slide down the mountain slope, covering everything, including climbers. At times we have been caught in violent snow storms that

buried our tents. During these storms, we could not get out and had to stay in our sleeping bags with all our coats and clothing on to keep from freezing.

But these are not all of the dangers. Wild animals also live on Mt. Ararat. The worst are the wild wolf-like dogs. These dogs are bigger than a German shepherd, but much meaner (and much uglier)! Many of the people living near the mountain will keep these mean, ugly dogs and train them to attack and even kill strangers. Several times we have been attacked. We have been thankful that we could keep them away with our sharp ice axes and by throwing rocks at them.

The north side of Mt. Ararat rises to 17,000 feet high.

Huge cracks, or "crevasses" in the mountain can be hidden by a thin covering of snow that is easily broken by a footstep.

STRUCK BY LIGHTNING

The hardest and most frightening adventure during our first search for the Ark happened as two friends and I were climbing near the top of the mountain. Many times on the mountain we have had to climb in snow storms, but this day there was a lightning storm! We were so high that we were actually up in the clouds. Suddenly, thunder hammered around us so loudly it almost made us go deaf. Rocks and boulders close by began making a humming noise. Electricity in the air made the hair on our heads, faces, and arms stand straight out. Then with a sudden blinding flash, all three of us were hit by lightning.

The lightning hit my body like a truck. The power of the lightning bolt threw me about 100 feet down the mountain. I landed on a steep rocky slope and then began rolling even farther down the mountain. As I fell, everything was black—I couldn't see and I didn't know what was happening. After rolling, bumping, and slamming into many big rocks, I finally stopped, and at the same time my eyes began to clear. I could see again.

For a few minutes I just lay in the snow, hurting all over. But when I tried to get up, I couldn't! The lightning had damaged all of the muscles in my legs and they wouldn't move. No longer were my legs strong, but now they were soft, like jelly. I called out to my two friends for help, but no one answered. Soon I saw that they also had been hit by lightning and were just as hurt as I was.

When the lightning hit us, we had already been climbing for two days and we were far away from our friends in the base camp lower on the mountain. Even if they came to look for us, there was no hospital nearby. All three of us were thinking that we were going to die.

PREPARING TO DIE

At that moment, I found that I wasn't afraid to die. Because I am a Christian, I knew that I would go to be with Jesus in Heaven if I died. Memories of when I was a child began flooding into my mind. As I lay paralyzed in the cold snow, I remembered when I was 5 or 6 years old with my father telling me stories about Jesus. It was one night, while sitting on his lap, I had asked Jesus to come into my life. As a child, I knew that I had been mean to my brothers and sisters, disobeyed my parents, told lies, and did other things that God calls sin. My father told me how Jesus Christ had come to die on the cross to save me from my sins. He told me how God would forgive my sins and come to live within me and help me to do the things that please Him. That night, I had asked God to forgive me

THE SEARCH GOES ON!

Since then, we have been back to Turkey and Mt. Ararat many times to look for the Ark. But there are many places on the mountain that the Ark could be. We have climbed to many of those places. We have studied pictures of the mountain taken from satellites in outer space. We have flown over the mountain in an airplane and a helicopter. Each time we learn more about the mountain, but we still have not found the Ark. Most of the searches were made when the Ark was probably covered by snow and rocks so that we could not see it.

Maybe someone else will find the Ark. My son Timmy wants to help me look for it someday when he gets to be a man, if it hasn't been found by then. Would you like to climb the mountain and search for the Ark? Now that you know the true story of Noah's Ark and what it looks like, maybe you can start your own expedition!

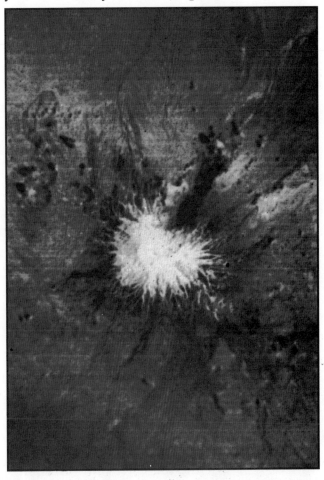

Satellite picture of Mt. Ararat, taken from outer space by LANDSAT.

for my sins and thanked Him for sending Jesus to be my Savior. From that time on I knew that I was a Christian, one of God's special children. And so, while I didn't want to die, I wasn't afraid.

But God had other plans than letting me die that day on Mt. Ararat. I began to recall Bible verses that I had memorized as a child —verses that said God can make a sick person well. I realized that God wanted me well again. He could make my legs strong again, just as easily as He made the lame man walk in the Bible.

And God did heal me as I prayed to Him. Soon I was walking around, taking care of my two friends, and before long, God made their bodies strong again too.

The storm still swirled all around us, with lightning striking everywhere, but we continued up the mountain to search for Noah's Ark. We praised God that He had worked a miracle that day to make us well.

CHAPTER 5

WILL GOD SEND ANOTHER FLOOD?

The Bible doesn't say that the Ark will be found. If someone does find it, pictures of the Ark will be in all the newspapers and on TV for everyone to see. But people do not need to see Noah's Ark to find Jesus and ask Him to save them from their sins. God has made Himself known to everyone through the Bible and also the things that He has made (Romans 1:20). The earth, outer space, the oceans, and all living things remind us that God is the One who made us—He is the One who is our King. And since God is King we need to obey Him. But people today can be just as sinful as the people in Noah's day. Because God hates sin and is a perfect Judge, He promises to punish sin just as He did with the people of the Lost World.

Will God send another Flood? No, God promised that He would never send another flood to cover the earth like the great Flood of Noah's day. But God still promises that those who disobey will be punished. The Bible teaches that "the wages (or penalty) of sin is death" (Romans 6:23). This kind of death is not only the death of our bodies. The Bible tells us of a place called Hell. Many times Jesus warned us that anyone who does not ask God to forgive his sins must go to Hell after his body dies. It is a terrible, hurting place away from friends, family and, most of all, away from Jesus, the One who made us and loved us enough to die for our disobedience.

THE GOOD NEWS!

But here is the good news! God does not want to punish those who have asked Him to be their Savior. We can enjoy Heaven with Him forever. Remember that when God punished the sinful people by sending the Flood, He gave them an opportunity to be saved. But only Noah and his family believed God and only they were saved.

In a very special way, Jesus Christ is like an Ark to us. The Bible says "the gift of God is eternal life in Christ Jesus our Lord" (Romans 6:23). We can live forever with God because "Christ died for our sins" (I Corinthians 15:3). Jesus Christ is God's Son. He never sinned, but chose to be punished for our sins instead of us.

Because He died on the cross, we do not

have to be punished for our sins. Just as Noah and his family were safe on the Ark, we can be safe with Jesus Christ as our Savior. "For God so loved the world that He gave His only begotten Son, that whoever believes in Him should not perish, but have everlasting life" (John 3:16).

The Bible promises that Jesus, our Creator, will come back and rule the earth some day. Again, the violent and evil people who hate God will die. Jesus will then change the earth back to what it was like before Adam and Eve disobeyed. Once again the earth will be a wonderful place. The people who have asked Jesus to save them from the punishment for their sins will live together in peace. There will be no animals that kill. Snakes that are poisonous will not harm, and lions, wolves, and bears will be tame. There will be no sickness and certainly no death or sin. Jesus Christ will be the King of all the earth.

And God said: "This is the sign of the covenant which I make between Me and you, and every living creature that is with you, for perpetual generations: I set My rainbow in the cloud, and it shall be for the sign of the covenant between Me and the earth. It shall be, when I bring a cloud over the earth, that the rainbow shall be seen in the cloud; and I will remember My covenant which is between Me and you and every living creature of all flesh; the waters shall never again become a flood to destroy all flesh. The rainbow shall be in the cloud, and I will look on it to remember the everlasting covenant between God and every living creature of all flesh that is on the earth."

Genesis 9:12-16 (NKJ)

42

A SPECIAL WORD

The Bible teaches us that we can pray to God and ask Him to forgive us for our sins and bring us into His loving family.

Prayer is simply talking to God. He hears you when you pray out loud or even when you think to yourself. He loves you very much. If you are ready to become one of His children, then here is a prayer that you could pray:

"Lord Jesus, I know that I am a sinner. I do many things that make you unhappy. Sometimes I disobey your rules, I am selfish and I want my own way. Dear God, I am sorry for these sins and I want to please you. I ask you to forgive me for my sins. I am thankful that Jesus loved me so much that He let Himself be punished instead of me. Please help me to obey you and live in a way that will please you. And thank you, God, for hearing me and for forgiving my sins. Amen."

DEDICATION

This book is dedicated to four very special people—my wife, Dalta, and my three children, Chara, Tim, and Beth, for whom it was primarily written.

ACKNOWLEDGMENTS

The author would like to express his deep appreciation to the following people, in addition to the artists listed below, for their assistance and support in helping make this project a reality: Dave Andersen, Mark Dinsmore, Robert Doolan, Bruce Hess, Jim Irwin, Elfred Lee, Dick Niessen, Don Shockey, Mary Thomas, and Dave Unfred.

ILLUSTRATIONS

Dave Andersen: i-1, 3, 18-19, 28A
Brian Bartlett: 38 (Climbers)
Ed Behling: 28F
Jonathan Chong: 2, 12-13, 16, 36-37, 40-41, 43
Eryl Cummings: 33
EROS Data Center: 37 (LANDSAT Image)
Dave GuMaer: 29C
High Flight Foundation (Courtesy NASA): 2
Ron Hight: 12, 14 (Ark with truck), 15, 20-21, 22-23
John Bultema: 35 (Crevasse)
Elfred Lee: 29B, 32,
John McIntosh: 26-27
Joe Morris: 30 (Ark in lake)
John Morris: i, 26-27, 34-35, 38, 38-39, 38-39, 39, 45
Wayne Ryther: 17
Doug Schmitt: 8, 14 (Stylized Ark), 24, 25
Al Shappell: 28E
Joyce Swiech: 22
Lester Walton: 28D
Jay Wegter: 6-7, 9, 10-11, 35 (Map), 42-43
Jim Wilson: 30 (U-2)

Book Layout: Dave Anderson, Jonathan Chong, Mark Dinsmore, Robert Doolan, John Morris
Cover Art: Dave Andersen